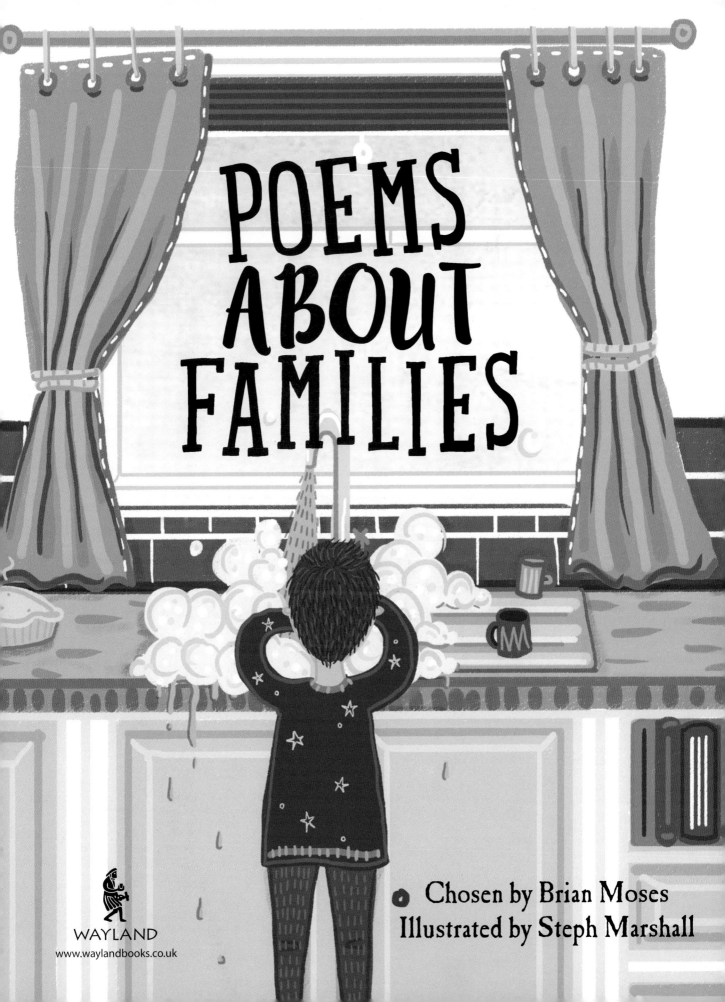

POEMS ABOUT FAMILIES

Chosen by Brian Moses
Illustrated by Steph Marshall

WAYLAND
www.waylandbooks.co.uk

First published in Great Britain in 2017 by Wayland
Copyright © Hodder and Stoughton, 2017

Editor: Hayley Shortt
Designer: Lisa Peacock

ISBN: 978 1 5263 0341 7
10 9 8 7 6 5 4 3 2 1

Wayland, an imprint of Hachette Children's Group
Part of Hodder & Stoughton
Carmelite House, 50 Victoria Emb
London EC4Y 0DZ

An Hachette UK Company
www.hachette.co.uk
www.hachettechildrens.co.uk

Printed and bound in China

Acknowledgements:
The Compiler and Publisher would like to thank the authors for allowing their
poems to appear in this anthology. Poems © the authors. While every attempt has
been made to gain permissions and provide an up-to-date biography, in some cases
this has not been possible and we apologise for any omissions. Should there be any
inadvertent omission, please apply to the Publisher for rectification.

'Waking at Gran's' copyright John Foster 1996 from 'You Little Monkey'
(OUP) reprinted by permission of the author; 'Like Who?' by Celia Warren,
first published in 'Cock-a-doodle-Moo' ed. John Foster (OUP 2001); 'Sister &
Brother' by James Berry from 'Only One of Me: Selected Poems by James Berry'
Macmillan 2004); 'Granny, Granny Please Comb My Hair' by Grace Nichols
from 'Come On Into My Tropical Garden' by Grace Nichols (Young Lions,
1988)

All websites were valid at the time of going to press. However, it is possible
that some addresses may have changed or closed down since publication.
While the Publisher and Compiler regret any inconvenience this may cause
the readers, no responsiblity for any such changes can be accepted by either
the Compiler or the Publisher.

Contents

Hands Up!

Hands up for your lovely Mummy!

Hands up for your lovely Dad!

Hands up for your lovely brother!

Hands down if they make you mad!

Hands up for your little sister!

Hands down if she growls at you!

Hands down for your older cousins!

Hands up if they play with you!

Hands up for uncles and aunties!

Hands down if they ask for a kiss!

Hands down for cleaning your hamster's cage!

Hands up if you love doing this!

Hands up for fluffy dogs and cats!

Hands up for all your pets!

Hands up for all your family!

Because family is

BEST!

Debra Bertulis

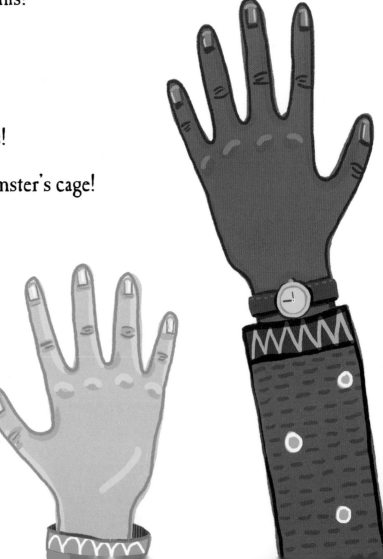

What are families for?

For giving, for caring,
for lending and sharing,
for pass-me-down-wearing,
families are for.

For telling, for hearing,
for clapping and cheering –
and sometimes oh-dearing!
That's what they're for.

For pulling together,
come fair or foul weather.
Yes, that's what they're for –
and more!

Kate Williams

5

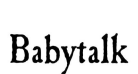

Babytalk

Baby screaming
"Waaaah! Waaaah! Waaaah!"
"Big sister's stolen my toy car!"

Baby wooing
Baby cooing
"Won't you tell me what you're doing?"

Baby bleating
Not so happy
"Somebody PLEASE – change my nappy!"

Gurgles, giggles
Baby mentions
"I love tickles and attention".

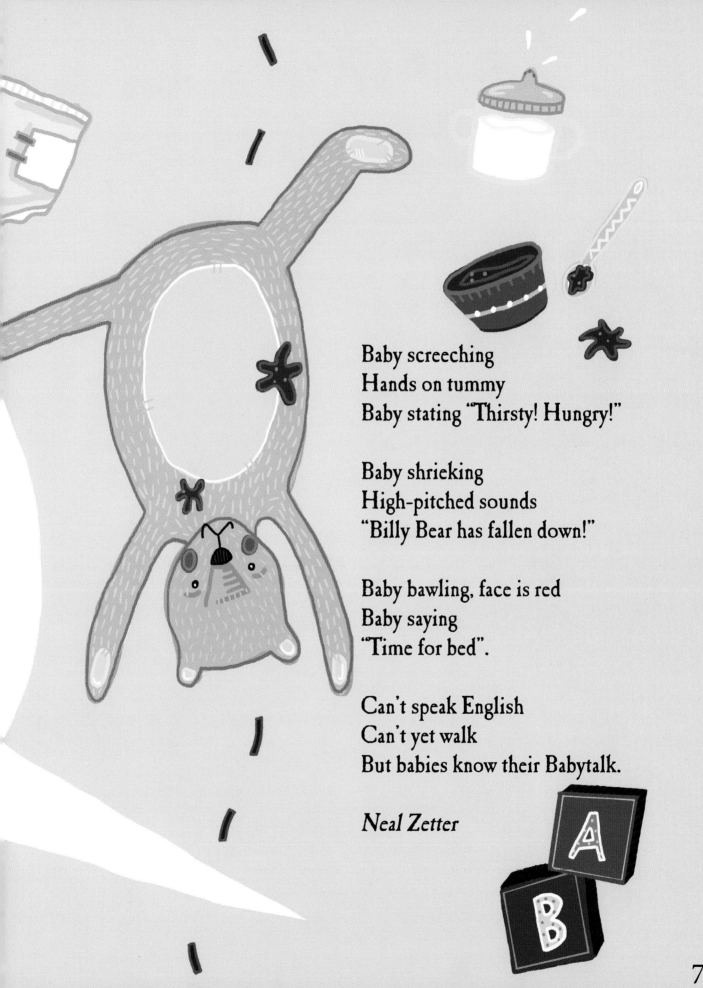

Baby screeching
Hands on tummy
Baby stating "Thirsty! Hungry!"

Baby shrieking
High-pitched sounds
"Billy Bear has fallen down!"

Baby bawling, face is red
Baby saying
"Time for bed".

Can't speak English
Can't yet walk
But babies know their Babytalk.

Neal Zetter

Mum's Shopping Day

Mum's going shopping,
(Moan, moan, moan).
Stops for a coffee,
(Groan, groan, groan).
Mum's choosing dresses,
(Loose, tight, long).
Tries some and buys some,
(Wrong, right, wrong).

I trudge behind her,
(Hot, cross, bored).
Dream of a castle,
(Draw my sword).
Fight with a dragon,
(Swish, swash, swish).
Steal all the treasures,
(Make a wish).

Prowl like a tiger,
(Flick my claws).
Howl like a wolf-cub,
(Lick my paws).
Snap like a crocodile,
(Chomp, chomp, chomp).
Stamp like a dinosaur,
(Stomp, stomp, stomp).

Bounce like a monkey,
(High, low, high).
Pounce like an eagle,
(Flip, flap, fly.)
Jump on a monster,
(Hip, hop, run) ...

Mum's looking grumpy –
I'm having FUN!

Clare Bevan

Adopted

I was adopted,
chosen with care
by a mum and a dad with love to spare.
They gave it to me.
Now we're together
and I have a family
for ever and ever.

Marian Swinger

Lucky Me!

Sally is my step-mum.
Mummy is my mum.
Both of them look after me,
and I look after them.

Gavin is my step-dad.
Daddy is my dad.
Never mind which one I'm with,
I'm always really glad.

I belong to all of them
and they belong to me.
I've got a double family –
what a lucky me!

Kate Williams

My Step-Dad

My Step-dad takes me to the park
He pushes me on the swing
And chats to me as we sit on the bench
About life and everything.

He says he really loves my Mum
And he really loves me too
And asks what I'd like for tea tonight
And if sausage and mash will do.

My Step-dad takes me to the park
We play as time flies by
My Step-dad is my second Dad
How lucky, how lucky am I?

Debra Bertulis

How Can I?

How can I wind up my brother
when I haven't got a key?

How can I turn on my charm
when I can't even find the switch?

How can I snap at my mother
when I'm not a crocodile?

How can I stir up my sister
when I'm not even holding a spoon?

How can I pick up my feet
and not fall to the ground on my knees?

How can I stretch my legs
when they're long enough already?

Parents! They ask the impossible.

Brian Moses

Puzzle

I thought I was the biggest child
in our little family,
but Mum says Dad's the biggest child
so where does that leave me?

Brian Moses

Like Who ...?

Grandpa says I've got Mum's eyes,
Mum says I'm like my dad,
Dad says his ears stick out too much
and mine are just as bad.

But when I look in the mirror,
all that I can see
is someone pretty neat and cool
who only looks like ME!

Celia Warren

Mum For a Day

Mum's ill in bed today
So I said I'd do the housework
And look after things
She told me it was really hard
But I said it would be dead easy
So ...

I hoovered the sink
Dusted the cat
Cooked Dad's shoes and socks in a pie
Washed up the carpet in the dishwasher
Fed the ornaments
Polished the fish, chips and mushy peas
Ironed the letters and parcels
Posted the shirts and knickers
And ... last of all ...
Hung the budgie out to dry.

It took me all day but I got everything finished
And I was really tired
And I'm really glad Mum isn't ill every day.
So is the budgie.

Paul Cookson

15

Sometimes

Sometimes he's a red Porsche 911,
Sometimes he's a fruit and nutcase from outer space,
Sometimes he's the lie that you wish was the truth
And sometimes he's ... the warmth inside a smile.

Sometimes he's the flip and jump in a seaside wave,
Sometimes he's a packet of crisps when you have toothache,
Sometimes he's the itch in the sand between your toes
And sometimes he's ... the twinkle in the black of a night sky.

Sometimes he's the exclamation mark in a sentence,
Sometimes he's a heavyweight boxing glove,
Sometimes he's a bag of multicoloured crayons
And sometimes, and best of all, he's simply ... my brother!

Ian Souter

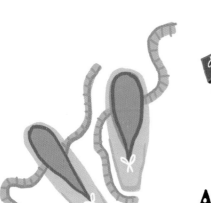

Twins

A poem for two voices

Voice 1	Voice 2
We look the same,	*but we're not one*
please use our names	*or we won't come*
we're not 'the twins',	*we're not 'you two'*
we're not at all	*dentical*
I like football,	*I love ballet*
I am quiet,	*I have my say*
We're not alike,	*don't dress us so*
we're not one half,	*you need to know*
we don't share heads,	*we don't share moods*
we don't agree	*on what tastes good*
I like pizza,	*I love a cake*
I hate cooking,	*I like to bake*

And though we share
there's two of us
don't send us gifts
don't spend double
I love puzzles
and where's the fun

the day we came
so two birthdays
for 'both of you'
just buy two
it's books I like
in half a bike?

There are some things
a secret place
but it's not fair
because we look
we are a pair
so don't call us

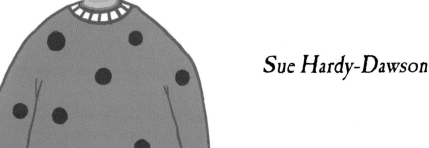

we love to share
some special words
to call us they
almost the same
but we're ourselves
the twins, OR ELSE!

Sue Hardy-Dawson

Our Jenny

Our Jenny has two half-length arms
that finish near her elbows,
but with one useful finger
and her thumb
she eats by herself,
plays games with me
and loves to read.

One of her legs is fine,
the foot a little twisted,
the other finishes in a knobby
lump just below the knee,
but Jenny swims happily
splashing and laughing
just like Mum and me.

My cheerful sister
with her pretty long brown hair
has long since stopped noticing
other children's stares
that follow her wheelchair everywhere
and seem to say,
'How would it be
if I were that way?'

Penny Kent

Sister and Brother

My sister sits
Like fallen feather in a chair
My brother tumbles in from upstairs

My sister speaks
For ears close in the room
My brother shouts through walls and rooms

My brother simply sits
And gets cross with his maths
My sister sails through her maths

My brother cooks
Like a four-star chef
My sister cooks and the food gets left

My sister waits on and on
Like a listening doctor
My brother jabbers through his teas and dinners

My sister sings the blues
My brother hurriedly pulls on
His running shoes

James Berry

Poor Grandma

Why this child
so spin-spin spin-spin
Why this child can't keep still.

Why this child
so turn-round
turn-round
Why this child can't settle down

Why this child
can't eat without getting
up to look through the window
Why this child must behave so I want to know
Why this child
so spin-spin spin-spin
Why this child
can't keep still

Grace Nichols

Laughter Lines

Gran has lots of little wrinkles
around the corners of her eyes.
When I ask her how they got there
she just looks at me, smiles and sighs,

They are formed from falling in love
and watching my family play,
new baby giggles, telling jokes,
waving from gates on first school days.

Every wrinkle tells a story
of fun filled birthday surprises,
wedding bells, Christmas presents,
silly Halloween disguises.

They are the result of tickles,
feel good movies that make me smile,
sharing old photos and stories
with friends I've not seen for a while.

Each of these lines is so precious
and such a special part of me;
A lifetime of love and laughter.
Every one is a memory.'

Julie Anna Douglas

Waking at Gran's

Sometimes,
When I stay at Gran's,
I wake up in the morning
And can't remember
Where I am.

I feel a moment's fear
That overnight
Someone has changed
The colour of the curtains
Re-papered the walls
And moved the door of the bedroom.

Then I hear Gran
Moving about downstairs
Chattering to the budgie,
As she makes my breakfast.

At once,
The world snaps into focus.
I know where I am
And that last night
I slept in the bedroom at Gran's
Where Mum used to sleep
When she was little
And my fear
Disappears.

John Foster

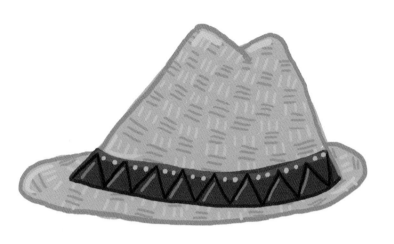

Changing Places

It's strange to think
that my Grandad
is *Dad* to Dad.

When *I'm* a Dad
will Dad be glad
to be *Grandad*?

Judith Nicholls

Cousins

Every evening
when the dark creeps in
like a smothering black cape,
our little family
– Mum, Dad, Brother, Sister, Gogo the cat and me –
we get together to huddle and cuddle
and keep us each safe.

Every night
when the moon rises like a white saucer,
our little family
– Mum, Dad, Brother, Sister, Gogo the cat and me –
go to bed in our warm rooms.
We tuck each other in
and sleep safe in green dreams.

But in another land,
when the same dark creeps in,
a broken family in a wild wind
looks to the same moon, red and angry,
and each makes a wish,
Mum, Dad, Brother, Sister, Asmara the stray dog
all ask for food, for medicine, for peace, for rain.

Just these, only these, do our beautiful cousins ask for.

John Rice

Further information

Once a poem in this book has been read, either individually, in groups or by the teacher, check with the children that they have understood what the poem is about. Ask them to point out any difficult lines or words and explain these. Ask the children how they feel about the poem. Do they like it? Is there a certain section or line of the poem that they particularly enjoy?

'Hands Up' by Debra Bertulis is a performance poem where one child reads the "Hands up …" lines and another child the "Hands down …" lines. Everyone else could raise or lower their hands according to what the lines demand. The "… and more!" at the end of 'What are Families For?' by Kate Williams, can also serve as a challenge to find further ideas. Note the words ending in 'ing' in the poem and see if others can be found.

Neal Zetter's 'Babytalk' is also a poem for possible performance. Can children think of other examples of 'babytalk'? Ask children from families that have a new baby in the house if they have experience of this.

'Mum's Shopping Day' by Clare Bevan is perfect for several voices. Perhaps an individual voice for the first line of each rhyming couplet and then several voices speaking the lines in brackets.

In my poem 'How Can I?' I noted down a few things that my parents used to say which I found puzzling. Perhaps children could choose one of the verses and illustrate their choice? Can they think of similar things that their parents say to them?

Does it annoy children when people tell them they look like a family member? Perhaps they could write their own poems in a similar style to 'Like Who …?' by Celia Warren. Paul Cookson's poem 'Mum for a Day' is a poem to perform with different voices speaking and acting out the bizarre things that happened when Mum stayed in bed for a day. Perhaps they could add strange ideas of their own.

Ian Souter's 'Sometimes' is a perfect poem to act as a model for children's own writing. They could write about other family members. 'Twins' by Sue Hardy Dawson is a performance poem for two voices. It can also lead to discussion about the fairness or unfairness of being a twin.

The last two lines in Penny Kent's poem 'Our Jenny' invite children to consider disabled children and attitudes towards disability. As always, look for the positive points in any discussion.

James Berry's poem 'Sister and Brother' is again a model poem for children's own writing. Ask them to list their own good and bad points alongside those of their brother or sister and to work them into a poem. Children without siblings could write about Dad and Mum or about themselves and a friend. Is there something that children do that annoys their parents or grandparents in a similar way to the girl in Grace Nichols' poem 'Poor Grandma'?

One of the lines in Julie Anna Douglas' poem 'Laughter Lines' reads, 'Every wrinkle tells a story'. Perhaps children could talk or write about the story behind a wrinkle on Gran's face? These could be real reasons or fictional ones. Are there children who often sleep in a different room and a different bed, as in John Foster's poem 'Waking at Gran's'? Do they feel something similar?

Most children will be aware of situations in other parts of the world where there are children who are not so lucky as they are. 'Cousins' by John Rice is perfect for encouraging a discussion about other countries where children grow up in a war zone, or experience natural disasters such as famines. Can we do anything for such children? How would children like to help them if they could?

About the Poets

James Berry was born in Jamaica, West Indies and came to Britain in 1948. He began writing when he worked as an international telegraphist for British Telecom. He is the author of a number of poetry collections and he won the Signal Poetry Award for his collection 'When I Dance' in 1989.

Debra Bertulis' life-long passion is the written and spoken word, and she is the author of many published poems for children. She is regularly invited into schools where her workshops inspire pupils to compose and perform their own poetry. Debra lives in Herefordshire where she enjoys walking in the nearby Welsh hills and seeking out second-hand book shops!
www.debrabertulis.com

Clare Bevan used to be a teacher until she decided to become a writer instead. So far, she has written stories, plays, song lyrics, picture books and a huge heap of poetry. Her poems have appeared in over one hundred anthologies, and she loves performing them in schools.

Paul Cookson has published over 60 collections and sold over a million books. He travels all over the world visiting schools to perform his poems. He is also the The National Football Museum's Poet-in-Residence. Although not very good at maths he has visited thousands of schools in the last twenty-seven years. His latest books are *Paul Cookson's Joke Shop* and *100 Brilliant Poems For Children*.
paulcooksonpoet.co.uk

John Foster is a children's poet, anthologist and poetry performer, well known for his performance as a dancing dinosaur. He has written over 1,500 poems and *The Poetry Chest* containing over 250 of his own poems is published by Oxford University Press. He is a former teacher and the author of many books for classroom use.
www.johnfosterchildrenspoet.co.uk

Sue Hardy Dawson has been widely published in children's poetry anthologies and her first collection *Where Zebras Go* is published by Otter-Barry Books. She has an open First Class Honours Degree and has provided workshops, both in schools and for the Foundation for Children and the Arts. As a dyslexic poet, she is especially interested in encouraging reluctant readers and writers.

Penny Kent: For many years Penny enjoyed teaching primary school children from thirty-six different countries at International Schools in Tanzania, Turkey, Germany, India and South Korea. The range of her cultural experiences is reflected in her children's poems, which have been published in many anthologies.

Brian Moses lives in Burwash in Sussex where the famous writer Rudyard Kipling once lived. He travels the country performing his poetry and percussion show in schools, libraries and theatres. He has published over 200 books including the series of picture books *Dinosaurs Have Feelings, Too* (Wayland) and *Lost Magic: The Very Best of Brian Moses* (Macmillan).
www.brianmoses.co.uk

Grace Nichols was born and brought up in Guyana. She is the author of several poetry collections for children including *Come On Into My Tropical Garden*, *Give Yourself a Hug* and *Cosmic Disco*. She lives in Sussex with her husband the poet, John Agard, and has two daughters.

Judith Nicholls started learning in a tiny one-room school in Lincolnshire. She has visited over 500 schools to run poetry performances and workshops with children and teachers. She loves gardening, walking, reading and having philosophical discussions with her

grandchildren. Her first book was *Magic Mirror* and since that she has written or compiled around fifty books.

John Rice has published seven collections of poetry for children and his poems have appeared in over 300 anthologies, magazines and newspapers. Several of his poems have been broadcast on the BBC and some have been set to music. He was Glasgow's Poet-in-Residence for two years during the Robert Burns 250th anniversary celebrations.

Ian Souter is retired from teaching and loves to exercise, play music as well as travel. He lives in the wilds of Surrey but also loves to visit, in particular, France and Australia. On his travels he keeps an eye (and an ear open) for words and ideas. Sometimes he finds them hanging from trees or people's mouths and also sparkling in the sunshine.

Marian Swinger was born in Lowestoft, Suffolk, but now lives by the Thames in Essex with her partner, son, dog and chickens. She has always loved to paint and draw and to write stories and poetry. She has been a professional photographer for most of her working life and has been writing poetry for children's anthologies for the past thirty years.

Celia Warren has written well over 100 books of children's stories, poems and puzzles. She grew up in North Lincolnshire, raised her children in the West Midlands, and now lives with her husband in South Devon. Ideas for her poems pop up at the oddest times from walking in the country to playing table tennis or line dancing.

Kate Williams: When Kate's children were young, she made up poems to read to them at bedtime. It was their clever idea that she send them off to a publisher, and she's been contributing to children's anthologies ever since! Kate finds writing a poem is like making a collage, but less sticky – except that she's stuck in the craze! She provides workshops for schools, too.
www.poemsforfun.wordpress.com

Neal Zetter performance poet, author and entertainer has been making people laugh through his poetry since 1989. He has starred in hundreds of West End comedy clubs, run his own club, appeared at the Royal Festival Hall, a League Two football match and at a funeral! His *Bees in My Bananas* won the 2015 Wishing Shelf Independent Book Award and 2016 saw his latest three books published by Troika with two more due in 2017. www.cccpworkshops.co.uk

Index of first lines